Father of two boys, and the second of six children of Dutch and Irish ancestry, Bruce Francis Schaafsma grew up on the North Shore of Sydney, Australia. He had a Christian upbringing which was heavily influenced by his parents and, in particular, his father, who worked tirelessly for the Saint Vincent de Paul whilst providing for his wider family and helping all those he could along the way.

Bruce has a commerce degree and is a Certified Practicing Accountant who has worked in various commercial environments and in hospitality for his whole working life. *Abundanomics – Unlocking the Real Wealth of Nations* is Bruce's first book, but he plans to contribute more in writing in the future.

Bruce Francis Schaafsma

ABUNDANOMICS – UNLOCKING THE REAL WEALTH OF NATIONS

AUSTIN MACAULEY PUBLISHERS™

LONDON • CAMBRIDGE • NEW YORK • SHARJAH

A CIP catalogue record for this title is available from the British Library.

ISBN 9781035826582 (Paperback)
ISBN 9781035826599 (ePub e-book)

www.austinmacauley.com

First Published 2024
Austin Macauley Publishers Ltd®
1 Canada Square
Canary Wharf
London
E14 5AA

To my parents whom I greatly admire for their strength, persistence, and patience.

I would also like to thank the resources of the world wide web and the Google search engine through which the task of sourcing, reading, and compiling information has been made so simple. Websites regularly used in research include (but are not limited to) Wikipedia, odometer, economics *discussion.net, ourworldindata.org, globalgoals.org, theatlantic.com, lifepersona.com, economics.harvard.edu, Merriam-webster.com/dictionary.*

Truly we are blessed with an abundance of readily available information.

To my friends and family who participated in the research, beta reading, and/or as sounding boards – thank you for your honesty, wisdom, and constructive thought.

Table of Contents

Introduction

Imagine if you could look at the world through a prism of abundance rather than scarcity.

The so-called "father" of Economics is the Scotsman Adam Smith. He wrote the book *"An Inquiry into the Nature and Causes of the Wealth of Nations"*, which is said to be one of the most important economic books of all time and was first published in 1776. His theories of economics have stood the test of time and his depiction of society being guided by what he termed the "invisible hand" is widely accepted. Smith considered man's primary objective is to guard his own interests above all others but, at the same time, be able to recognise the need to offer or accept help and cooperation from others. Although the quote "greed is good" is widely attributed to the Hollywood movie "Wall Street" it was, in fact, Adam Smith who coined the term "greed is good".

Following on from this, the most widely accepted and recent definition of economics is:

'Economics is the science that studies human behaviour as a relationship between end results and scarce means which have alternative uses.' This definition was formulated by Lord Robbins in 1932.

From that definition, the following propositions were derived:

- Human wants are unlimited; wants multiply – luxuries become necessities. There is no end to wants. If food was plentiful, if there was enough capital in business, if there was abundant money and time, there would be no scope for studying economics.
- The means or the resources to satisfy wants are scarce in relation to their demands. Had resources been plentiful, there would not have been any economic problems. Thus, scarcity of resources is the fundamental economic problem for any society. Even an affluent society experiences resource scarcity. Scarcity gives rise to many 'choice' problems.

This definition and its subsequent propositions are now nearly 90 years old, and much has changed in the intervening years.

- Do these fundamental ideas, that are taught everywhere, still hold true?
- Does an environment underpinned by the idea of scarcity, and fuelled by associated emotions, encourage selfish behaviour both on an individual and a systemic level?
- Does the assertion that things are scarce drive an environment of greed, where it's every man for himself, a kill or be killed mentality, where only the strong survive?

- Has the education system worldwide evolved to reflect the bewildering amount of change in the fundamental nature of our society since the Industrial Revolution?

For thousands of years, in a broad sense, a self-centred mindset was the only choice. You lived and died by your ability to satisfy your needs and that of those who were important to you.

However, the renowned British economist John Maynard Keynes (1930s), when reflecting on the extraordinary rate of development in Europe and the United States, suggested that "the economic problem" might actually be "solved" by 2030. Essentially, he was saying there would come a time when we could afford to shift our attention from the advantages of greed to the disadvantages of greed.

Is the notion of scarcity, at least in a macro sense, still valid today? Or do we now have the choice to view the world as abundant, with plenty to satisfy the needs and wants – at least at a basic level – of all people, no matter what their race, religion, or socio-economic background happens to be their fortune?

'Imagine all the people sharing all the world'
John Lennon / Yoko Ono

Chapter 1
Evolution

Since people started to think they started to create. Whether you believe in the evolutionary theories of Darwin or those of Creationists, need has always been the mother of invention.

For many, the progression of the world from one age to another might seem like the natural order. Others would offer an alternative view, arguing that choices have always been made with causal effects. Furthermore, they would assert that the ability to make decisions, to shape our future, is in our hands more today, than ever before in history.

From early cave men's drawings to the advent of Gutenberg's press, from the evolution of the wheel and engine to the development of the banking and finance sector, the human mind, and its creative nature, have led us to the world we have today. The accumulation of these inventions, as well as many other innovations and discoveries, has seen humans evolve from hunter-gatherers to a generation of tech-savvy individuals with few barriers to accessing and developing all parts of the world.

Let's look at some of the most important discoveries over the course of history and how they have helped to usher humanity into new ages, making the world a better place for many of its inhabitants.

Game Changing Inventions and Discoveries

- **Fire** – imagine being alone in a shelter surrounded by a forest, with no electricity and no sources of light. When night comes, it's pitch-dark; you are left at the mercy of nature and any nocturnal creatures lurking around, posing the threat of destruction or even death. For early people, life was even worse than that scenario. There were no houses to hide in or doors to keep predators out. The places they stayed in were open to attack from anything and anyone. Even if predators could be held at bay, there were natural forces to contend with, such as cold, bad weather, volcanoes and earthquakes delivering disaster directly to their door. Early people had little respite except, most often to curl up in the nearest corner and hope for the best.

  The discovery of fire would have been life-changing, and the importance of its discovery to humanity cannot be overstated. Fire changed the way early people hunted and gathered food. It provided warmth and light, upgraded their defence systems, improved their diet, and extended the hours during which activities could be carried out beyond sundown. Fire laid the groundwork for many subsequent innovations.

- **Iron** – the discovery of iron was so pivotal to human evolution that historians named the period in which it was discovered the Iron Age. While the period differs considerably across regions, its significance remains constant. The Iron Age marks the point from which iron was first discovered and effectively replaced bronze as the primary source of tools and weapons. This was recorded to be around the 12th century BC. Iron is said to have been first discovered accidentally by people in West Africa and Southwest Asia around 1500 BC. This discovery, however, didn't reach Europe for another 500 years or more. By the time it did, it had completely revolutionised the world. Iron technology worked wonders in the creation of tools, weapons, and industries, and it is no surprise iron has remained an integral part of human society to this very day.

- **The Wheel** – The world didn't know what the wheel was until the ancient people of Mesopotamia invented it around 4200–4000 BC. However, wheels made during that period weren't used for transportation; they were primarily used in the creation of pottery and ceramics.
  Although unknown at the time, these early forms of the wheel represented a ground-breaking template for the creation of transport. Wheels ultimately helped usher in the better and more efficient movement of goods, services, and people. Wheels helped to create wealth and opened the door to a myriad of

possibilities for subsequent innovations, which are now an integral part of the world as we know it today.

- **The Engine** – It's only fitting to discuss the impact of engine invention alongside commentary on wheels. The invention of the wheel was crucial for enabling humans to move from one point to another using horses and other animals to push and pull material and people around. The engine effectively made transportation easier and faster. The rise of engines took the use of the wheel to another level.

  The very first known prototype of an engine has been traced back to about 400 years ago. The advent of engines made it possible to travel overseas by boat or plane covering distances over short periods of time, that only a century earlier would have been only a pipedream. These days the development of steam engines, internal combustion engines, diesel engines and turbine engines of all sorts means that goods, services, and people can be transported to almost any part of the world virtually overnight.

- **The Printing Press** – The world has undergone considerable change since the emergence of the Industrial Revolution around 1760. Significantly, it evolved into a knowledge-based environment with a greater emphasis on gathering knowledge and applying our understanding of that knowledge to invention and innovation. This change is why many regard Gutenberg's printing press as one of the world's most important inventions. Without the printing press, man would have found it impossible to spread knowledge in a timely and easy manner available for all people.

Before Gutenberg's Press came into being in the 1450s, the art of printing had long been a Chinese forte; they had been printing for nearly a thousand years using the woodcut technique. This method, invented during the Han Dynasty, involved using a block of wood to create relief patterns on silk, the first known printing medium.

With literacy booming in the 1430s, there was an imbalance created by there being many who were interested in learning and the relatively small amount of printed material available. Johannes Gutenberg recognised this imbalance and worked hard to create the printing press to increase the availability of books and promote literacy. Leveraging his knowledge of metallurgy and goldsmithing, Gutenberg developed letter moulds, which remain perhaps his most significant contribution to the art of printing.

The advent of the printing press led to a surge in literacy, especially amongst commoners. News travelled faster and research became easier to carry out. Such was the esteem in which Gutenberg's press was held that his methods remained largely unchanged for over 300 years.

The ability to disseminate information has been dramatically enhanced over the last 40 years with the development of the internet, email, and SMS messaging. Large volumes of information can now be delivered quickly and easily to people around the world. Further, people anywhere in the world can now access endless amounts of information on any subject, almost instantly. Again, this is something no one would have thought possible just a century ago.

- **Banking and Currency** – Banking has been a part of our societies for as long as printed currencies have existed, and perhaps even before that, in various forms. It all began with the need for traders to pay for their goods and services with something universally acceptable as payment. Initially, printed bills were the most widely accepted form of payment, but they were soon replaced by coins made from various metals. With faster transportation in place, better trades and more prosperity, the need for secure places to store wealth emerged.

While most homes did not have places considered safe enough to keep their wealth, available records show that some elites – particularly in the Roman Empire – stored their assets in temple basements where the presence of priests were deemed sufficient to ensure their safety. These records also show that some of these temples loaned out money stored in their care and made profits in the form of interest charges.

Medieval banking was quite crude in the way it operated. Modern banking was first introduced, in theory, in 1776 by the Scottish economist Adam Smith. He introduced the idea which argued for an economy free of government control. That was the beginning of modern banking as we know it today.

Since then, the banking industry has evolved and has kept evolving to suit the needs of the society it serves. These days huge amounts of wealth can be transferred anywhere at any time, payments for delivery of goods and services can be electronically transferred in a secure and timely manner. The ability to carry out these types of transactions, that we consider standard today, was far more difficult and time consuming only a few generations ago.

- **Aviation** – For thousands of years, people have marvelled at birds and wondered how the mysteries of flight could be harnessed for human endeavours. Birds have been honoured, revered, and worshipped in various cultures throughout history. They possess many qualities that may have seemed supernatural or God-like to ancient civilisations. In Egyptian theology, we have Horus, the God of War and Sky, depicted as a falcon-headed figure. From Aztec history, there is Huitzilopochtli, the God of War, depicted as either an eagle or a hummingbird. The Thunderbird, from Native American lore, is represented in totem poles. These are but a few examples from cultures around the globe.

  Regrettably, the first significant application of human flight is so closely related to warfare.

  In 1903, the Wright brothers demonstrated that an aeroplane could sustain controlled flight. Merely ten years later it was weaponised for use in World War One.

Nevertheless, the invention of manned flight has profoundly transformed the world and the 20th century saw remarkable progress. Just 66 years after the Wright brothers' historic flight, humans landed on the moon. Moreover, advancements in aeroplane technology, from propeller-driven to supersonic, have enabled goods, services and people to be transported across the globe in hours rather than weeks or months.

- **Nuclear Energy** – This technology utilises the energy released by splitting the atoms of certain elements, most commonly uranium. It was initially developed in the 1940s, and during the Second World War, research predominantly focused on bomb production. However, by the 1950s attention had shifted towards the peaceful use of nuclear fission for power generation.
From 1945 onwards, efforts were made to harness this energy in a controlled manner for naval propulsion and electricity generation. Since 1956, the prime focus has been on the technological evolution of reliable nuclear power plants. From the late 1970s to about 2002 the nuclear power industry, despite improvements in safety and output, suffered some decline and stagnation in use and uptake.
In the early 21st century, several factors combined to revive prospects for nuclear power. First was the realisation of the scale of projected increased electricity demand worldwide. Secondly was the awareness of the importance of energy security – the

prime importance, for each country, to have assured access to affordable energy. Thirdly was the imperative to limit carbon emissions due to concerns about climate change.

Nuclear energy currently provides about 10% of the world's electricity, generated from approximately 445 power reactors. Nuclear is the world's second-largest source of low-carbon power. At present, over 50 countries utilise nuclear energy worldwide.

- **The World Wide Web** – Tim Berners-Lee, a British scientist, invented the World Wide Web (WWW) in 1989 while working at the European Organisation for Nuclear Research. The Web was originally conceived and developed to meet the demand for automated information-sharing between scientists in universities and institutes around the world.

  By 1995, with the release of Windows 95 and the popular Internet Explorer browser, it became apparent to most publicly traded companies that having a public web presence was no longer optional. Initially, people saw the main possibilities being that of free publishing and the instant provision of information worldwide. However, increasing familiarity with two-way communication over the web led to the possibilities of direct web-based e-commerce and instantaneous group communications. This combination of more user-created or edited content and the easy means of sharing content has led to many sites adopting the style we typically see today. These sites have articles with embedded video, user-submitted comments below the article and RSS (information sharing and page update) boxes to the side.

The development of the internet has been achieved in the last thirty years – the world is virtually unrecognisable, in this sense, to the one in which our grandparents grew up.

The Current State of Play

There are many other inventions that could be included and discussed. The combination of these examples, and that of many others created from human imagination, brings the ability to achieve even greater things:

- Developments in the areas of the engine and energy have enabled us to distribute goods and services quickly and efficiently anywhere in the world.
- Advances in communications mean we can distribute information rapidly and efficiently anywhere in the world.
- Developments in the banking and finance sector mean we can distribute wealth quickly and efficiently anywhere in the world.

We have an abundance of all these resources. These three key elements are here, in the world today, in abundance, for all of us to see and to leverage for everyone's benefit.

Further these channels of distribution are available and unparalleled, at every level, in the history of the world as we know it. They are pathways to unlock a better world for everyone.

A world where the ability to allocate and distribute resources worldwide is no longer a problem.

This level of abundance calls into question one of the great underlying premises for the study of economics.

We no longer live with the constraints of 18th or 19th or even the early 20th century thinking.

The world has taken huge steps forwards in the last century, and as a result, so too must our education system.

One of the most fundamental ideas in economics, that of resource scarcity and the associated ability to distribute, should be challenged and discussed.

Chapter 2
Resources

There are many examples of renewable resources or, for all intents and purposes, unending and abundant resources.

Solar energy, water, air, and even human resources are all present in this world in plentiful supply. Human intellect and 'brain power' exist today like never before, especially given the population explosion we experienced in the 20th century, which has continued into the 21st century. These resources are all abundant and serve as the foundations for all life on this planet; they are virtually unending in their supply. That is, unless we cause irreparable damage to our world through nuclear or climate-related disasters, but I will comment on those issues later.

We are currently at a juncture, in the history of earth, where we have the ability to create a better place for everyone.

Renewable Energy

To put it simply, renewable energies are those from sources without a known finite end or those that are reusable, primarily from natural sources. Typically, when we hear the term "renewable energy", we immediately think of solar power, wind power, and hydropower and yet, they are not the only sources.

Energy plays a huge part in our everyday lives: our electronic devices need electricity to power up, our streetlights need it for illumination, and our vehicles run on diesel and petrol. In our homes, we use oil, gas, and electricity for lighting, heating, and powering our devices. These energies drive commerce, manufacturing, and business of all types.

Before the Industrial Revolution, the bulk of energy used for light and heating was sourced, bar an exception or two, from renewable sources. Primarily, however, it was the discovery of coal that fuelled the Industrial Revolution. This subsequently led us to the extraction of oil in enormous quantities, which accelerated the invention of technologies that propelled us into the 20th century.

The discovery and use of fire parallels the history of civilisation and is the first significant application of renewable energy for the advancement of mankind.

For most of our existence, we made use of what is now known as biomass (including plant materials like grass, wood, mosses, etc.) to fuel our fires. These were vital sources of power and the fireplace was the central element to most homes until recently.

Our ancestors continued in the same fashion for many thousands of years before oil was discovered. Other ancient sources of energy included animal power as well as wind for a sail which helped humans engage in distant trades for over 8,000 years. Hydropower, such as with the use of dams to trap water and turn it into energy is also well-established in human history.

We have known since early stages of the mass mining of coal and oil that there would eventually be a peak, followed by a subsequent time when these resources ran out.

The concept of peak oil in the 1950s began a new drive towards renewable energy sources. Solar, hydro, and others energy sources were seized upon by both environmentalists and industrialists. They were equally concerned about the exponential growth in human population and in oil and coal consumption. They realised these resources are finite and that they will run out regardless of the size of the supply today. A growing environmental movement, the development of environmental sciences and a push against pollution meant that more than ever renewable energy became not just a scientific innovation for the future, but a necessity.

In the 1970s, we began to look back at some of these ancient methods and technologies to provide the power sources of tomorrow. Theories about when we would reach peak oil and coal consumption were being discussed as early as 1870. Remarkably, even during the Industrial Revolution, some visionaries were theorising about and developing concepts of solar technology to prepare for a post-oil and coal world. The reasons and timelines may have changed but the thinking has not; many modern technological developments are aimed at a world without reliance on oil and coal.

Energy security has been a major concern for world leaders since the latter part of the 20th century, and even more so since the beginning of the 21st century. The term refers to the link between each country's national security and the availability to that country of resources for energy production and consumption. If a country loses access or finds it has restricted access to oil and other resources, instability is likely to occur as energy is rationed. Energy security concerns could be the result of armed conflict or political instability in coal, gas or oil producing countries. Or perhaps, as a result of, a buying country having access restricted when a producing country deliberately cuts supply.

The fundamental reason for these behaviours lies in the scarcity of these finite resources. Greed, or a view that there is a need to be self-centred drives these decisions. The belief they only have the capacity to look after themselves means people outside of their circle of interest are of no concern and, as a result, should fend for themselves.

Energy security is essentially another way of saying we believe we don't have enough. We are going to protect our supply, our livelihood, we are choosing to be selfish. We are making a logical decision that anyone thinking through a prism of scarcity would do. Very logical from that point of view. But are there alternatives? Is there a source of energy that is endless?

Our energy comes from the sun, one way or another!

In the pre-industrial age, solar energy met all of humanity's energy needs. Plants convert solar energy into biomass through the process of photosynthesis. People burned this biomass for heat and light. Additionally, plants provided food for people and animals, which in turn used their muscle power for work. Even as humans learned to smelt metals and make glass, they fuelled the process with charcoal made from wood. Apart from photosynthesis, humans made some use of wind and waterpower, also ultimately fuelled by the sun.

Temperature differences in the atmosphere brought about by sunlight drives the wind. The cycle of rainfall and flowing water also gains its energy from sunlight. The sun is at the centre of all these systems. However, in the past, people could only use the energy that the sun provided in real-time, storage of the energy, apart from using fossil fuels, was a massive barrier for mankind.

In 1900, roughly 50,000 horses pulled cabs and buses around the streets of London, not to mention carts for transporting goods. As you can imagine, this created an enormous amount of waste. As Lee Jackson writes in his book "Dirty Old London", by the 1890s, London's immense horse population generated roughly 1,000 tonnes of dung per day. The manure also attracted flies, which spread disease. The transportation system was literally making people sick. The pre-fossil fuel era was not the utopia we might have envisaged. Clearly, we cannot transition our world back to those days particularly in light of the worldwide population explosion.

Fossil fuels opened new doors for humanity. The transformation of ancient plants through pressure, temperature, and time essentially stored the sun's energy. The resulting fuels freed humanity from its reliance on photosynthesis and biomass production as its primary energy source. Fossil fuels allowed the use of more energy than real-time photosynthesis could provide since fossil fuels represent a stored form of solar energy.

First coal, then oil and natural gas allowed rapid growth in industrial processes, agriculture, and transportation. The world today is unrecognisable from that of the early 19th century before fossil fuels came into mainstream use. Human health and welfare have improved markedly, and the global population has increased from 1 billion in the year 1800 to almost 7.5 billion today. The fossil fuel energy system is the lifeblood of our modern economy. Fossil fuels powered the industrial revolution and lifted millions out of poverty but has also created poverty on a scale never previously experience.

Renewed Growth in Renewables

According to reports from the International Energy Agency, the amount of electricity produced from renewable sources was projected to increase from 13% in 2012 to 26% by 2020.

In terms of total energy generation, renewables account for 19% of our present-day usage. These figures are encouraging, and most long-term forecast models predict that the use of renewables will triple between 2012 and 2040.

Domestically, the US produces just over 13% of its electricity from renewable sources. It is one of the world's largest consumers of energy and consumes around 25% of the world's energy production each year.

The exponential economic growth in China, and the equivalent exponential growth in coal mining, means that China is the number one consumer of energy in the world.

At the same time the Chinese state-owned utility company, Huanghe Hydropower Development, has finished building the world's largest solar power project in a desert in the north-western Chinese province of Qinghai. In fact, China leads the world as the top producer of solar energy, followed by the United States, India, Japan, and Vietnam.

In 2015, a United Nations report concluded that renewable technology is now being produced on an industrial scale which bodes well for the future. However, even though it is a worldwide concern, clearly the US and China need to join forces to resolve the very important issue of sustainability for future generations.

We are well on our way to harnessing renewable energies and creating a world that can be powered by an endless, renewable, and abundant sources of energy.

It is, however, a far more difficult process when economic notions of scarcity and greed are embedded in the hearts and minds of decision makers.

Water Resources

Have you ever been to the beach and marvelled at how much water you can see? Have you ever been in an aeroplane and noticed that the world is mostly covered by water? In fact, the world is 75% covered in water. There is no shortage of water on earth. The earth boasts water bodies including the oceans, lakes, and rivers that stretch across approximately two-thirds of its surface.

So why do we still have people in this world without access to clean drinking water? Why are people dying of thirst or diseases spread from polluted water sources?

We have known for thousands of years how to remove salt from water to make it fit for human consumption.

The process of desalinating seawater to make it drinkable has a long and rich history. Some of the earliest instances of desalination in history date back to experiments by Aristotle some 2,400 years ago.

Typically, the places that utilise desalination the most are dry and arid countries like Saudi Arabia, United Arab Emirates, and Israel. Notably, these are countries are of great wealth, and perhaps ironically, mostly derived from the proceeds of fossil fuel production. With current technology, clean, drinkable water can be delivered to people everywhere.

So why haven't we fixed the problem? We have the technology, the wealth, the distribution channels, and an abundance of the basic water resource. The issues can be "distilled" into one idea that keeps resurfacing – many people are self-centred and self-interested no matter what spin they like to use in their rhetoric.

Ideals that drive self-interest have been reinforced throughout history and are now an unquestioned part of the curriculum in our education systems at almost every level throughout the world.

Globally, there are approximately 16,000 operational desalination plants located in many countries. These plants generate an estimated 95 billion litres of freshwater per day. Many of these are micro-desalination plants which operate near natural gas or fracking facilities in the United States, and they are arguably environmental hazards.

Thankfully, there have been very positive developments in this area with environmentally friendly and sustainable desalination processes such as solar dome technology showing promising signs.

However, the thing that is blatantly obvious from the list of desalination plant locations, is the absence of desalination plants in the worlds' hungriest, thirstiest and most undeveloped countries as follows:

Nigeria – no desalination plants
Afghanistan – no desalination plants
Lesotho – no desalination plants
Sierra Leone – no desalination plants
Liberia – no desalination plants
Mozambique – no desalination plants
Haiti – no desalination plants
Madagascar – no desalination plants
Timor-Leste – no desalination plants
Chad – no desalination plants

Currently, there are 786 million people worldwide without access to a safe drinking water source. In other words, 10% of the people in the world are constantly thirsty and desperate for access to one of the most abundant and fundamental resources we have on Earth.

And, as usual, it's the countries that need it the most that have it the least. Some of these countries are landlocked and perhaps problematic from a technology point of view. However, we pump, pipe, and ship coal, oil, and gas many thousands of kilometres all around the world when we think it important. Aren't the poor people important enough?

Given the wealth in the world these days, can we hear ourselves saying these two opposing positions are reasonably justified without being conflicted or choking on our own words?

The idea that the "big economic problem" is the allocation of scarce resources is questionable to say the least. Perhaps we should study our world as a glass half full rather than half empty.

Perhaps we are now at the time where we can look at the world through educated, abundant eyes instead!

What else do we have in abundance in the world today?

Chapter 3
Population

By the end of the 21st century, the human population is expected to have reached at least 10 billion. It's incredible to think this possible, especially since there were only 170 million of us 2,000 years ago. Currently, we stand at just over 7 billion people. This population boom, particularly over the last 300 years, shows little sign of slowing.

The causes and effects of uncontrolled population growth should be of great concern to us all. Are there too many people? Are there enough resources for everyone to live a reasonable life? How are we going to manage this incredibly large issue without ignoring it or pretending that, because it doesn't affect me, that it doesn't exist?

A Brief Look at The History of World Population

It may not be apparent or present in our daily thinking, but our current and projected population figures are living proof of the resilience of humanity and what humanity has been able to achieve over time.

Humanity has had to battle wars, natural disasters, diseases, and, of course, death, to reach this point. Great leaps of progress and population growth have been achieved whilst enduring massive setbacks including:

- The Mongol invasion of China in the early 13th century (said to have claimed the lives of tens of millions of humans).
- The Black Death, which spread all over the world, killing over 95 million people (over 25% of all people worldwide) when world population was just around the 350-million mark.
- Numerous wars, which have been consistently recurring throughout history and include two world wars in the 20th century.

On top of all this, major natural disasters recorded in history include tsunamis, floods, earthquakes, volcanic eruptions, cyclones, and plagues (including the recent COVID-19 pandemic). All of which have proven to be little more than a speed hump to growth in population worldwide.

In fact, since the commencement of the covid pandemic, the world population has increased by approximately 150 million, or approximately 210,000 people a day.

Humanity is not at risk of extinction from the COVID-19 pandemic. In Australia, for example, the total number of deaths in 2019 (before Covid) was 169,301 and was more than (by 28,185) the total deaths in 2020 which was 141,116 despite the "ravages" of the pandemic.

Perhaps there are far greater issues in the world today, such as:

- How are we going to feed, accommodate, and clothe all these new people?

If we put aside the subjective issue of whether COVID-19 is the most important issue facing the world today and consider the coronavirus pandemic now compared to years past – in past years we would have been helpless, watching as the virus claimed lives without mercy as it swept through nations.

It is a credit to humanity that we have been able to apply ourselves, to the point where we can approach health challenges, such as pandemics, and work collectively to find answers quickly to such threatening circumstances.

Imagine if we applied ourselves as willingly to resolving the problems of death by starvation and thirst as we have to the issue of COVID.

Recently, in November 2021, there was a world climate summit in Glasgow, Scotland, which is a great and positive sign for the future health and sustainability of the world.

Why isn't there a world "Overpopulation and I'm Dying of Starvation and Thirst" summit? Surely this should be equally, if not more, urgent.

There are a variety of factors that have led to humanity's recent population boom which is now multiplying like a mathematical equation on steroids. Let's look at a few of the factors, and some examples, of where population growth has exploded, subsided, or even gone backwards.

The Industrial Revolution

The Industrial Revolution played a significant role in the population explosion of the last 260 years.

The transition from a primarily agricultural society, that worked primarily with manual labour, to a world leveraging off inventions and fossil fuels has led to the production of everything, including people, increasing at rates never previously seen in the history of mankind.

The Industrial Revolution began and ended at different times in different parts of the world, yet its effects were broadly much the same everywhere. Early industrialists remained agriculturalists but they were able to do so on a much larger scale. They worked with machines that helped to increase productivity on farms. Further they worked with machines that helped to process and utilise agricultural by-products to create better yields.

The rise of large factories led to a movement of population away from rural areas to urban situations as the job skill requirements of the new age changed. Improved technology, coupled with a larger and improved labour force, meant more goods and services could be produced for consumption, trade, and storage.

One of the consequences of the increased availability of goods and services was that people lived longer and populations increased. As populations grew, so too did the demand for goods and services and for larger labour forces. Much like the proverbial snowball getting bigger and bigger as it rolls down the hill – it is difficult to stop once it gains momentum.

Broadly speaking, as conditions improved, populations increased both in terms of birth rates and of expected life span.

However, as these new technologies brought great wealth to some, they did not do so to others. Many people were, and are still, being exploited in the process and are forced to live in conditions at or below the poverty line. In essence, people were, and still are being "kept" by the wealthy for as long as they prove useful.

Of course, these oppressive "human" characteristics are not new and slavery, for example, existed well before the Industrial Revolution and is well-documented.

A more recent example of exploitation is of African people in diamond mining for the benefit of rich and supposedly civilised people.

The film "Blood Diamond", starring Leonardo DiCaprio, depicts this type of exploitation and, whilst it is not a documentary, it is fundamentally based in truth. In fact, it also highlights the exploitation of children forced to become child soldiers. Unbelievably, there are an estimated 400,000 child soldiers in the world today – some as young as eight years old.

It is ironic to note that whilst deserved attention is brought to the exploitation of the poorest amongst us via the Hollywood entertainment production line, the wealthy have found another avenue for procuring riches far beyond what they will ever need and with little discernible improvement in the conditions of those exploited.

So, in short, with the advent of the Industrial Revolution came the possibility of the exploitation of the growing population for greed and wealth on a much larger worldwide scale.

Scientific and Medical Advancements

Another factor leading to the population explosion was that as information was more widely available, research and development was heavily leveraged and shared. This led to a significant leap and expansion of knowledge across the globe.

With greater knowledge, more widely distributed, more people were able to develop scientific, technological, and medical solutions to problems that were formerly thought to be insurmountable to humanity.

The globalisation of knowledge, although slow at the start, meant that many parts of the world developed in tandem.

As one solution was being applied in one location, word quickly travelled and soon, if it was thought to be of value, was adopted elsewhere.

This is primarily how it became possible for humanity to address previously insurmountable diseases and premature death. Antibiotics like penicillin saved millions of people from untimely death. As diseases and premature deaths were tackled head-on by medical innovations, people began to live longer and heal from illnesses that would have claimed their lives in earlier times.

The average lifespan in England in 1700 was 35 years; now, only 321 years later, it is 82 years. Average lifespan in China in 1700 was less than 25 years, and now, only 321 years later, it is 77 years.

It is comforting to note we, at least, have a sharing nature in the area of science and medical advancement.

Population Explosion and Why It Is Accelerating in Some Places and Slowing Down in Other Places

The Chinese Example

When the word "overpopulation" is mentioned, many people immediately think of China – not all that surprising, really. China has a population of about 1.4 billion people now compared to 400 million in 1900. China is currently home to the highest single concentration of humans in the world. All this despite the many millions of lives lost during the Communist and Cultural Revolutions between 1935 and 1966, and the one and two-child policies which have been place since 1980 until recently.

The population of China has, until recently, been in what would have seemed an uncontrollable upward spiral. Now, however, projections suggest it will plateau or even decline in future years. China is considered a developing country in some respects, but in other respects one of the richest countries in the world.

One might surmise that as wealth and quality of life improve then birth rates decrease.

The African Example

The thing about population explosion is that it has different dynamics for different places. In Africa, the current population is about 1.1 billion people. It is the fastest-growing continent and is expected to surpass the 2 billion mark by 2050. By 2100, the continent is expected to add another 500 million people to that number. Countries like Tanzania, Ethiopia, the Democratic Republic of Congo as well as Egypt are expected to join Nigeria in the top 10 most populous countries in the world.

There are several reasons for the population explosion in Africa. These include adherence to certain religious beliefs, lack of education, poverty, and, more positively, an improvement in the continent's health sector, which has seen the death rate reduced in certain areas with people living longer.

Of these factors, the relationship between poverty and birth rates is of particular interest:

- Why is it that people who are poor typically have larger families than those who are wealthy.
- Why do we generally see an inverse relationship between income and fertility rates?

In short, the higher the degree of education, standard of living, and the production of goods and services per person, the fewer children are born per person or family.

Karan Singh, a former minister of population in India, illustrated this trend by stating, 'Development is the best contraceptive.'

The Relationship Between Population Growth Rate and Poverty

Africa has a legion of governmental and non-governmental organisations scattered across the continent. They are all trying to address the issue of curbing population growth by family planning in various ways. They are hoping to help reduce the continent's population projections as they continue to grow at alarming rate

The effort is extremely admirable but as the saying goes – "hope is not a strategy".

Recent statistics show that 689 million people (predominantly children, young people, and especially women) live below the extreme poverty line globally. Much of that figure is concentrated in crisis-ridden regions like Syria and Yemen, while African countries south of the Sahara Desert also suffer, with 40% of its inhabitants managing on less than $2 daily.

It is reported that 1.3 billion people are living in multidimensional poverty in 107 developing countries of the world. Of these numbers, African countries still have the highest poverty rates in the world.

Amongst the consequences of poverty is the number of people who die as a result of the lack of access to affordable healthcare – this is estimated at 10,000 per day or 3.6 million per year.

Further, an annual figure of 100 million people are forced into extreme poverty because they cannot afford healthcare.

Further still, thirty-five thousand people a day or nearly 13 million people a year die of starvation worldwide – to put it into context that is more than half the population of Australia or North Korea or Chili or Cameroon or Romania each year!

Can you imagine dying of starvation?

In contrast, the world's richest 1%, sitting at the very top of the economic pyramid, have **more wealth than over 6 billion** other people combined.

Between 2018 and 2019, victims of world hunger increased by 8.9%, even though the amount of food produced on the planet is enough to feed everyone. Seven hundred million people across 43 countries currently suffer from scarcity of water – a basic requirement to live and a resource we have in abundance!

Clearly, the disparity between the "haves" and "have not" is an untenable situation for the world both from the point of sustainability and from a humanitarian point of view.

From a sustainability perspective and in "economic" terms, if population growth were to slow, then so too would demand for the products that the world provides. The incessant need to rape and pillage the finite resources of the world would diminish.

Currently we are in the midst of a mass extinction of species and alarming deforestation rates caused by humans. If it continues, the planet will lose vast ecosystems and the essential commodities they provide, including fresh water, pollination, pest and disease control. Essentially, we are eroding the capabilities of the planet' to sustain human life.

We cannot allow the population of the world to spiral uncontrollably as it is, can we? Surely, we cannot stand by and watch as millions of people and species of all kinds continue to perish when we have the ability to help.

We have in our hands now the wealth and the ability to resolve these issues!

A fundamental shift in the way we think and educate is required to address these issues. A redistribution of wealth is clearly required.

Raising the minimum living standards of everyone in the world, whilst still giving incentive to people who achieve and contribute more, should and could be the goal for all of us.

There are examples of this ideology scattered all through the world. In Australia, for example, there is a safety net for all people in the health care sector that gives everyone access to quality health care and that is supported by all the Australian people.

When there is so much of every fundamental resource, in abundance, in the world, it should not be too much to ask for it to be distributed more equitably!

Further, and importantly, it is not necessary to completely strip the wealthy of their wealth to raise the living standards of all mankind – there is more than enough for everyone.

Now is the time for us to reach a collective epiphany:

Greed is not good, greed is unnecessary!

Chapter 4
Wealth and Poverty

Distribution of wealth is the process in which the wealth is shared amongst the people.

Currently, in the world today, there is a chasm in terms of the gap between the rich and the poor, and it's getting worse with the rich getting richer, and, of course, the poor are getting poorer!

It is blatantly unfair, inhumane, and unnecessary to horde most of the wealth between so few. As mentioned earlier:

- In 2017, approximately 1% or 75 million of the 7.5 billion people in this world owned 50.1% of the world's wealth. This was an increase from 45.5% in 2001.
- In 2017, the total wealth of the world was estimated at $280 trillion, with $140 trillion owned by only 1% of the people.
- In 2021, the total wealth of the world was almost $420 trillion – a 50% increase in only four years!

Despite a generally well-meaning education sector and various religious institutions, their message is falling flat.

They tell us, and our children, that "sharing is caring" and that we should be good and take care of our fellow man. That message is clearly falling on the deaf ears of many of the people with wealth and power.

Could it be that our education system is sending mixed messages? Care and share on one hand and, on the other hand, be self-involved and self-interested. Is our desire for massive consumption and personal possessions driven by our education system? An educations system which is arguably largely built on the economic premise that the greatest problem humanity faces is the allocation of scarce resources.

Are the deadly sins of greed, pride, and envy winning over the virtues of charity, humility, and kindness? There is no end of charitable organisations doing wonderful things in our world, but the issues of overpopulation, death by hunger, thirst, and curable disease continue to persist.

Imagine if 20% of the wealthy people's wealth from 2017 figures ($28 trillion) could be redistributed to the dying, starving, and needy people of the world. And why not? The rich don't need it; they have enough to live many, many lifetimes over as it is!

What does $28 trillion (just 20% of the wealthy's wealth) buy?

- 112,000 medium-sized desalination plants, or 568 for each country in the world. Water problems solved everywhere many times over!
- 248,889 medium to large new hospitals for every country in the world. Health issue worldwide resolved everywhere!

Of course, you don't need that many desalination plants or hospitals to deliver basic services to everyone. You may argue about the price or the technology, but the point remains that there is still plenty of financial resources left over to resolve and explore many other issues on top of these.

Other issues, such as perhaps 35,000 people per day dying of hunger worldwide.

Above are some examples to illustrate how ludicrous the situation has become! Here are some more examples of extraordinary wealth beyond any single human's need.

Extreme Wealth

- **Elon Musk** owns and runs various companies such as Tesla, Space X and is said to be the richest person in the world. He is a South African born American entrepreneur. Musk is well known for Brands such as Pay Pal and Tesla motors. Musk is also well known for his quote, 'when something is important enough, you do it even if the odds are not in your favour.' His $204.2 billion net worth is equivalent to $11.1 million for <u>every day</u> of the rest of his <u>expected</u> life.

- **Bernard Arnault** is the wealthiest European in the world. His net worth is estimated to be $187.9 billion. His father made a small fortune in construction; Arnault got his start by putting up $15 million from that business to buy Christian Dior in 1985. He oversees 70 well-known brands, including Sephora, Christian Dior, and Louis Vuitton. Louis Vuitton is the world's largest luxury goods company. His wealth decreased by $30 billion last year after the purchase of luxury goods went down due to the COVID pandemic. However, by August 2021, the sale of luxury goods had surged, which saw him become the wealthiest man in the world with an estimated net worth of $198.4 billion. He is an investor, businessman, and art collector and his wealth continues to increase as the value of his portfolio of investments grows. His $187.9 billion net worth is equivalent to $39.6 million for every day of the rest of his expected life.

- **Gina Rinehart** is Australia's richest person, with a net worth of $31 billion and. She is the Executive Chairman of Hancock Prospecting, a private company involved in mineral exploration. The company has continued to grow due to the increasing size of the market for Australia's iron ore in China. Her personal wealth increased by $2.2 billion in just six months which led her into attaining the $31 billion net worth. Her family alone is worth $40 billion, which is double the amount of the individual following her in the list of Australia's richest people. Her biggest source of income is in the trading of iron ore with China. Her wealth continued to grow despite the COVID pandemic. Her $30 billion net worth is equivalent to approximately $4.8 million for every day of the rest of her expected life.

- **Aliko Dangote** is the richest person in Africa with, has a net worth of $12.1 billion. He owns a business empire named the Dangote Group, which he started 30 years ago. Dangote Group and which is one of the largest employers in West Africa. The business mogul started by borrowing $3000 from a relative immediately after completing school at the age of 21. He used the money to import agricultural products, which he sold in Nigeria. Within three months, he had repaid the loan and further expanded his business to selling cement. He has held the title of the richest man in Africa for the last ten years. Dangote was entrepreneurial from a very young age, and he has gone ahead and partnered with the Bill and Melinda Gates Foundation to help eradicate polio in the region. He has also started an oil refinery in Nigeria, which is Africa's largest industrial project. He runs multiple businesses across various industries including oil, sugar, consumer goods and manufacturing. His $12.1 billion net worth is equivalent to approximately $1.6 million for every day of the rest of his expected life.

- **Jack Ma** is a Chinese business mogul and philanthropist. He is a co-founder of the technology company Alibaba and Yunfeng Capital, a private equity firm. He believes in an open market economy contrary to what is happening in his country as the trade war between China and the United States continues. In an open market economy, the government does not try to control what is happening in the market by imposing restrictions such as price caps. He is also the third wealthiest person in China, with a net worth of $51.5 billion. Jack Ma retired as the executive chair of Alibaba in 2019 and moved to further his education, philanthropy, and environmental causes. Zhang Daniel took over the position of executive chair at

Alibaba. His $51.5 billion net worth is equivalent to $5 million for <u>every day</u> of the rest of his <u>expected</u> life.

Contrasting this:

Extreme Poverty

- It costs just under $2 per day to keep people in third world countries above the international poverty line, according to the World Bank.
- Each year, 12.7 million people per year, in the world, die of starvation.

To prevent these deaths, a redistribution of $9.2 billion (less than 1%) per year, out of the 28 trillion previously mentioned, would prevent millions of painful and horrible deaths. Clearly, it's within our means and collective budget.

There is plenty of wealth to go round but, despite constant well intended effort, there appears to be no real appetite for fairer distribution of wealth.

The bottom line is, there is plenty of wealth to go around, but how do we get people to realise that, in an abundant world, there is no need for greed.

The World Bank uses three poverty lines for global poverty comparisons, where $1.90 per day is the international poverty line, $3.20 per day for lower-middle poverty line income countries, and $5.20 per day for upper middle poverty line income countries.

The American standard to feed a person per day is $11.40. The poorest in the most downtrodden situations don't need even close to that. An increase of say double, from $1.90 per day to $3.80 a day would improve their situation immeasurably and is affordable!

The African continent has some of the poorest countries in the world. These countries include Madagascar, which has a 70.7% poverty rate, Guinea Bissau with 69.3%, and Eritrea with 69%. Being poor means that the individual lacks enough money to cover their basic needs and sometimes individuals can go for a long time without food, shelter, and clothing.

Many people in Africa are so poor that they cannot afford school fees and in return lack formal skills for employment. Often children have to walk for long distances to get to school and, as a result, don't always attend.

- On average, they "live" on less than $1.90 per day compared with the average of the wealthy, listed above, of $3.1 million per day.

India has many millions of people who live in extreme poverty. The World Bank defines an individual living on less than $1.90 to be poor. With less than $1.90 in a day, it is impossible to get adequate food, shelter, and clothing. Most people live in informal settlements that are overcrowded putting them at very high risk of diseases. Those who are fortunate enough to find work end up spending almost their entire daily income on basic needs. India also has very strong cultural norms that tend to favour the men over the women; hence most of the girls end up without formal education. Without formal education, women have difficulty supporting the home financially and need to rely on the income of the husband. Many Indian girls are also married off at a very young age, thus denying them the chance of pursuing other opportunities.

- On average, they "live" on less than $1.90 per day, compared with the average of the wealthy, listed above, of $3.1 million per day.

Canadian Aboriginals are a native group of people living in Canada. During the colonial times, the land belonging to these Indigenous people was taken away by the Europeans, and the people were consolidated in villages. The land belonging to these people was fertile and the Europeans needed the land to grow crops and feed their growing populations, so they just took it. Aboriginal children were also taken away to ensure they did not learn the cultural ways of their ancestors. Most of these people do not have formal education which means they do not have enough skills to take up existing jobs in the market. Many of them survive by begging on the streets. They are often accused of being thieves because of their lack of jobs and skills. These people often live in large groups and share rental fees as they cannot afford to rent out houses as individual families.

- On average, they "live" less than $5.20 per day, compared with the average of the wealthy, listed above, of $3.1 million per day.

Many **African Americans** are amongst groups considered extremely poor. These people were originally displaced, from their African homelands to various places, including the United States during the slave trade. They were mistreated as they worked long hours with little or no pay. After the abolition of the slave trade, they remained mostly in the United States and were still considered to be a lesser group, hence, could only find the manual jobs that paid little. For many years, these people were still not allowed to live in the same estates as the white people, nor could their children go to the schools belonging to the whites. The racial segregation of generations greatly affected their financial status. With limited income, many of these people were unable to access formal education. This cycle has continued from generation to generation such that it has become imbedded in their culture.

- On average, they "live" on less than $5.20 per day, compared with the average of the wealthy, listed above, of $3.1 million per day.

Mexico has a huge income gap leading to high poverty levels that can only be dealt with by taking proactive steps towards closing the gap. Approximately 6 million people live on less than $2.00 a day, and another 37.6 million people in Mexico live on less than $5.00 day. There are two groups of poor people in Mexico – those living in extreme poverty and the rest who are moderately poor. The poverty levels in Mexico have been measured based on parameters, such as access to clean water, nutrition, health care, education, shelter, and social security. Most people in Mexico lack access to healthcare, formal education and healthy meals. The medical facilities are few as compared to the population size.

The health system lacks modern medical equipment which is used in treatment of diseases such as cancer and kidney failure. Without access to basic services such as healthcare, it is difficult for many individuals to find regular work. Many people are still unable to provide shelter for their families. Many schools are in poor condition and many families cannot afford school fees.

- On average, they "live" on less than $3.20 per day, compared with the average of the wealthy, listed above, of $3.1 million per day.

Maslow's Hierarchy of Needs

Abraham Maslow described, in 1943, a hierarchy of need that has three distinct levels.

The first is referred to as the basic level. Why can't we aim to have everyone, worldwide, living at what he terms the basic level? That is, everyone has enough food, water, warmth, and they feel safe and secure.

Surely not a target that anyone could argue we shouldn't set as an objective – raise the minimum standard of living worldwide.

Arguably, this would have the complementary effect of slowing population growth. There would still be scope in Maslow's hierarchy for people who want more to achieve more. We have the wealth and the technological ability at our disposal today, so why don't we?

Motivation and Charitable Organisations

Many charitable organisations have stepped up, either on the international stage or in their various regions. Many of these organisations are committed to putting an end to the idea of individuals living on less than $1.90 per day and have come to play a significant role in trying to curb wealth inequality in the world.

The United Nations, which no doubt is well intended, has played a significant role to make sure countries, and their people, are protected by the rule of law. However, the United Nations does not have the power to totally interfere in the constitutions of sovereign states, therefore, lacks the ability to enforce standards. This is particularly true if the people in power, in the country of interest, do not care to listen.

Another charitable body is the Bill and Melinda Gates Foundation. This is a non-profit organisation that has been giving aid and grants to developing countries, helping to empower youths, especially in Africa. The foundation provided an endowment / donation fund of $49.8 billion in 2019.

These are all highly motivated groups of people, but are they swimming upstream? Swimming against a raging current, in a world conditioned to greed being the primary motivator? Are the poor merely feeding off the scraps of the rich?

This greed, fuelled by a history of need and re-enforced in almost every school, college, university, and educational institution worldwide, is clearly no longer necessary.

Imagine a world without greed, what would that look like?

Chapter 5
Belief

We don't have to try very hard to imagine a world without greed as being a positive thing – we believe it!

There isn't a major religion that promotes ideals of greed or selfish behaviour. In fact, and perhaps unsurprisingly, it's quite the opposite. The truth is the major religions promote ideals of sharing and caring for each other and are similar in that they portray the world, through its abundant resources, as capable of taking care of all who live upon it.

Following are some, but not nearly all, illustrations of this mentality from major religions throughout the world:

Abundance in Christianity

The Christian religion portrays God as the God of abundance. As the "Creator" of heaven and earth, He is seen as abundance personified. With God, Christians believe that, as long as they put their trust in Him and live their lives according to His will, they will receive all that they need and whatever they lack will be attended to.

It is in this context that the God of the Christian faith is referred to as "Jehovah Jireh", which translates to "Our Lord

Provider". A corresponding text from the Bible, the Holy Book of the Christian faith, says of God as the ultimate provider:

'But my God shall supply all my needs according to his riches in glory through Christ Jesus.' (Philippians 2:19)

In the Bible, both Old and New Testaments, there are examples of events that corroborate the idea that things are abundant in the world.

- <u>Kings 17:3</u>

It didn't rain for three-and one half years. During this period there was famine, and it was said God would provide for Elijah. Initially, he was being fed by ravens with meat and bread. The waters of the creek soon dried up and he was directed by God to go to a certain widow at Zarephath where he would be fed. The widowed prepared food and drink for him first and then for herself and her child. Despite the famine in the land she always had plenty.

- <u>Exodus 16:35</u>

Abundance was demonstrated in the story of the children of Israel having left the shores of Egypt for the *"promised land"*. On their way to the promised land, they had to pass through the wilderness. They ended up moving from one point to another for 40 years without securing a permanent place to live. However, during this period, they lacked for nothing, they had an abundance of food.

- <u>Matthew 15:32–38</u>

Here, Jesus was on a mountain by the sea of Galilee.

There he taught and healed the sick for three days. After the third day he saw the people were hungry and thirsty. He asked his disciples how they could feed them. The disciples were perplexed and replied that it was impossible to find that much food in such a wilderness area where they were. Jesus then asked how many loaves of bread they had in their midst, the disciples then discovered that they had seven loaves of bread and a few fish. On giving these items to Jesus, he gave thanks and broke the bread and gave it to his disciples to distribute to the people. At the end, all the people were fed with seven more baskets of leftovers. The number of them that ate were more than four thousand men, women and children.

- <u>Luke 5:4–7</u>

When he had finished speaking, he said to Simon, 'Put out into deep water, and let down the nets for a catch.' Simon answered, 'Master, we've worked hard all night and haven't caught anything. But because you say so, I will let down the nets.' When they had done so, they caught such a large number of fish that their nets began to break. So they called to their partners in the other boat to come and help them, and they came and filled both boats so full that they began to sink.

These stories, and many others, portray abundance for people of good will who know where to look and how to share. These miracles demonstrated that adherence to

Christian values is directly correlated to abundance, in all things, for all people.

Abundance in Islam

Miracles of abundance are also recorded in Islam. While the Prophet Muhammed (PBUH / Peace Be Upon Him) was alive, many of his deeds and miracles of divine acts were recorded by his companions, mainly by the "Seven Abdullah's".

According to Islamic tradition writings, Sahih al-Bukhari and Sahih al-Muslim testified about the Prophet Muhammed (PBUH) miracles of the abundance of things:

- Abu Ayyub al-Ansari had hosted the Prophet Muhammed (PBUH), and said, 'I made a meal sufficient for two people – God's Messenger and Abu Bakr. The Prophet, however, told me to invite the distinguished Ansaris (Helpers). Thirty men came and ate. He then told me to invite another 60, which I did. They also came and ate. God's Messenger also told me to invite more, which I did. They came and ate. There was still food left in the bowl when they finished eating. After witnessing that miracle, all who had eaten took the oath of allegiance. One hundred and eighty men ate food prepared for two.'

- This report is found in both Sahih al-Bukhari writings and the Muslim Book of Traditions, which were related by Abd al Rahman ibn Abu Bakr. He said, 'We had 130 Companions, accompanied by God's Messenger on an expedition. Dough from four hundred handfuls of wheat was prepared to make bread, a goat was slaughtered and cooked, and its liver and kidneys were roasted. I swear by God that God's Messenger gave each of us a piece from the roasted parts and put the cooked meats in the bowls. We ate until we were full, and still, there was some leftover. I loaded it onto a camel.'

- This report is found in both Sahih al-Bukhari writings and the Muslim Book of Traditions, which were related by Abd al Rahman ibn Abu Bakr. The food was cooked in my house. And after everyone ate and left, the pot was still boiling with meat, and bread was still being made from the dough. God's Messenger had put water from his mouth into the dough and the pot, and then prayed for abundance.'

- Sahih al-Bukhari and Sahih al-Muslim share that during a feast of the Prophet's marriage to Zaynab, Umm Sulaym (Mother of Anas) did fry a handful of dates and then told Anas to take them to the Prophet. Anas did this and the Messenger of God told him to invite whomsoever he saw to the Prophet's house. Anas did as he was told, and the people he invited were 300 hundred in the Prophet's room. The Prophet then said they should sit in circles of ten, afterwards, he humbly prayed on the food and directed that it be shared amongst the people, and the people ate to their satisfaction. Anas then cleared the tables, when he did so Anas testified that, 'I could not tell if there was more food when I set out the dish or when I removed it.'

It is clear these passages are remarkably similar in meaning to those mentioned earlier in Christianity.

Following are the six major beliefs in Islam:

- Belief in the Oneness of God: Muslims believe that God is the creator of all things, and that God is all-powerful and all-knowing. God has no offspring, no race, no gender, no body, and is unaffected by the characteristics of human life.

- Belief in the Angels of God: Muslims believe in angels, unseen beings who worship God and carry out God's orders throughout the universe. The angel Gabriel brought the divine revelation to the prophets.

- Belief in the Books of God: Muslims believe that God revealed holy books or scriptures to a number of God's messengers. These include the Quran (given to Muhammad), the Torah (given to Moses), the Gospel (given to Jesus), the Psalms (given to David), and the Scrolls (given to Abraham). Muslims believe that these earlier scriptures in their original form were divinely revealed, but that only the Quran remains as it was first revealed to the prophet Muhammad.

- Belief in the Prophets or Messengers of God: Muslims believe that God's guidance has been revealed to humankind through specially appointed messengers, or prophets, throughout history, beginning with the first man, Adam, who is considered the first prophet. Twenty-five of these prophets are mentioned by name in the Quran, including Noah, Abraham, Moses, and Jesus. Muslims believe that Muhammad is the last in this line of prophets, sent for all humankind with the message of Islam.

- Belief in the Day of Judgment: Muslims believe that on the Day of Judgment, humans will be judged for their actions in this life; those who followed God's guidance will be rewarded with paradise; those who rejected God's guidance will be punished with hell.

- Belief in the Divine Decree: This article of faith addresses the question of God's will. It can be expressed as the belief that everything is governed by divine decree, namely that whatever happens in one's life is preordained, and that believers should respond to the good or bad that befalls them with thankfulness or patience. This concept does not negate the concept of "free will"; since humans do not have prior knowledge of God's decree, they do have freedom of choice.

Except for the fact that Christians believe Jesus is the son of God, not just a prophet, and that Christians don't read scripture from the Quran, there is more that Christians have in common, than not, with Islamic beliefs.

There are approx. 2.2 billion Christians in the world. There are at least 1.9 billion people of the Islamic faith. That is, at least, half of the world's population agree on many more fundamental beliefs and ways to behave than they disagree.

Are these religions basically in accord with other religions?

Abundance in Hindu and Buddhism

Unlike the demonstrations of an abundance in the Abrahamic religions, Hinduism and Buddhism do not readily make available documented examples of supernatural manifestations of abundance.

Perhaps part of the reason for this is because, unlike the Abrahamic based faiths, Hinduism is not dependent on one single figure or founder but is considered a philosophically rich way of life for its followers.

However, in Hinduism, there is a goddess of wealth, power, fortune, beauty, and fertility called "Shri Lakshmi". According to Hinduism, she holds the promise of contentment and material riches in her hand, and she is ready to bless all her subjects.

Hindu worshipers invoke her in the following way:

'Beautiful goddess seated on a chariot,
Delighted by songs on lustful elephants,
Bedecked with lotuses, pearls, and gems,
Lustrous as fire, radiant as gold,
Resplendent as the sun, calm as the moon,
Mistress of cows and horses,
Take away poverty and misfortune.
Bring joy, riches, harvest, and children.'

In Buddhism, the founder and leader of this religious sect, Guatama Buddha, was reported to have performed miracles, but none included miracles of abundance.

The Buddhist view is that charity as an act is meant to reduce personal greed which is an unwholesome mental state that hinders spiritual progress. A person who is on his way to spiritual growth must try to reduce his own selfishness and his strong desire for acquiring more and more.

Despite the relative lack of empirical evidence to support the supernatural manifestations of miracles showing abundance, the belief that there is enough to take care of everyone in the world is a part of both the Hindu and Buddhist faith.

Collectively Hindu and Buddhists account for approximately 2 billion of the world's population.

The four religions mentioned account for, and represent, approx. 80% of the world's population.

The Jewish faith account for a further 18 million and are of similar fundamental beliefs as they too emanate from the Abrahamic linage in the company of Christian's and those of the Islamic faith.

Commonality of Belief

The barriers to building a richer, fairer world for all are man-made and could be summed up in three words – ego, pride, and greed.

All the religions mentioned demonstrate goodwill and brotherhood. This is largely because the foundation of religion is based on social unity and forging a way of helping each other.

The elements of how that goodwill and brotherhood are shown can vary from one religion to the other.

The Christian principle of goodwill and brotherhood is based on brotherly love which was demonstrated many times by Jesus Christ.

In Islam, it is seen in their communal way of life. Brotherhood and goodwill are often demonstrated in cultural ways, such as dress, festivities, and worship.

The Islamic religion, by virtue of the Quran, believe in goodwill and brotherhood towards one another, and it is expressed in the holy text in various passages:

- 'And as for those who strive in our path – We will surely guide them in our ways. And indeed, Allah is with those who are of service to others.' (Al-Qur'an 29:70)
- 'Indeed, Allah is with those who are righteous and those who do good.' (Al-Qur'an 16:129)

It is evident that the concept of abundance, brotherhood, and goodwill is a common feature of religions despite the nuances in how they are presented.

Of course, some of these illustrations may be difficult to accept literally, or even on face value, by some. Debate will continue about the validity of the various religious texts. People will refer to other documented texts to discredit or divert discussion; however, the ideologies of liberality and benevolence are common to these religions.

If we know where to find abundance and how to distribute abundance, then surely we should share it, as there is plenty for everyone. This ideology is generally true of all religious beliefs and does not contradict any substantive theology. It would be generally true no matter what a person's culture or particular background might be.

And, of course, as illustrated throughout this book, we have abundance in all things right now in the world today. We have ways to distribute it and, as discussed, the fundamental belief that it is the right thing to do.

Realisation of the truth is the only missing piece. A change in mindset, via a fundamental restructuring of elements of the education system, is overdue.

When you look at the world through the prism of abundance, it is abundantly clear that the time is right for a redistribution of wealth in a fair and equitable way to create a more peaceful culture and a more loving, inclusive world.

Chapter 6
Culture

Values, Similarities and Differences

So, as we can see there are many fundamental similarities in religious belief across various backgrounds worldwide, even when the religion originates from different sources.

In fact, people worldwide have more culturally in common than they have differences.

Maslow's Hierarchy of Needs presents the idea that everyone in the world aspires to have, at least, the basic needs of food, water, and warmth in order to lead a happy existence.

Further to this, Maslow describes psychological and self-fulfilment needs to which people can still aspire which are above the basic needs.

If the basic level was able to be delivered to all people, there would still be room for motivated people to aspire to higher levels. There would be many people who would be happy to live their lives at just the basic level, having all their basic needs met, and still live a good and satisfying life.

If everyone is fundamentally happy and has their needs met then what need is there for war?

Typically, war is driven (initially) by a sense that one or more parties are feeling that they are being unfairly treated. That is, the other party, or parties (to the war) have been greedy and are exerting their will in an unfair or aggressive manner. This may just be a perception, but fair or not, a conflict arises. People will ultimately rise in anger at the harsh circumstances in which they find themselves if circumstances deteriorate enough.

What we see in developing and developed countries is, that when the environment is sufficiently good, we rarely see uprising of any significant note. The real instability in the world comes from third world or early stage developing countries. It seems logical that the pathway to a peaceful world is to distribute abundant resources more evenly. Being fed, warm, loved, and sheltered takes the sting, or the ill feeling, out of any conflict. Most people don't want to fight. Most people want to be happy, but sometimes they are driven to fight by circumstances.

There is no need for greed in a world with so much abundance. With a fairer distribution of wealth, there would be little need for war. People would, at the very least, be comfortable enough. Further if we created a vision so that people could improve their lot in life then people could strive for betterment, or not, as they choose. If you give everyone the same access to opportunity, then it will depend on the person as to what they do with that opportunity.

World Issues in Context

Just like life is known to have ups and downs, the history of human existence has been laced with episodes of great progress and tranquility and other periods of disasters and emergencies.

Catastrophies are not new and have even been mentioned in the Bible such as the great floods during Noah's time. There have been two World Wars, the Black Death, the Spanish flu, and the Great Financial Depression of 1929.

However, in equal measure, humans have had triumphs such as the invention of the steam engine that spurred mechanisation and the Industrial Revolution, the signing of the Human Rights Declaration by countries under the UN, and humans space flights to the moon and others mentioned in the earlier chapter on Evolution.

Recently the human race, has been caught in yet another so called crisis COVID 19. But is it really the biggest issue facing the world today?

Amplifiying the impact of COVID-19 is the "big" topical and emotionally charged discussion around climate change.

The world is being overwhelmed by the news of extreme weather phenomena across the globe. The most current form of extreme weather is the "out-of-control" wildfires across the world's forests and natural habitats. This is occurring in unprecedented regions such as Siberia, whose average temperatures have warmed up by about 2 to 4 degrees celsius from climate change over half a decade. While the wildfire seasons (especially in the US, Canada, and Australia) are usually considered normal and anticipated, the current fires are larger and spread faster. Turkey and Greece have also recently experienced intense wildfires to which they are unaccustomed – so much so that they required international help to fight the fires.

Recent years have seen record high numbers in temperature, rainfall, hurricanes / cyclones and tornadoes – or more generally in extreme weather events.

It would seem that COVID-19 and climate change together would be the most urgent issues needing to be addressed in the world today. It is a hard case to argue against...

But are they? The world has dealt with major diseases and pandemics before! The world has adapted to climate change before. We cannot ignore these issues but are there other big issues not entirely present in our everyday thought or in the media?

Are we being led by the "news" which is full of negative characterisations of the world? Surely, there are positives we can focus on. What is the benefit, or purpose, of distracting the people with all the negativities?

In the last one hundred years alone, the human race has faced and managed to adapt to many catastrophes and upheavals:

- The Russian Revolution
- World War One
- The Spanish Flu
- The Great Depression
- The Chinese Revolution
- The Second World War
- The Korean and Vietnam Conflicts
- The Cold War and Nuclear Threats
- AIDS
- Various Recessions and Global Financial Crises

With all that on our collective résumé, surely, we will navigate our way through the current "so-called" major issues facing humanity.

Consistently, throughout the last one hundred years, the world population has been increasing at alarming rates – surely this should be front-page news every day! There are some 150 million more people in the world today than when COVID-19 first appeared. Further, because of inequalities, many are in urgent need and are dying horrific deaths from starvation, thirst, and curable diseases.

Discussion of inequality is not just a first-world topic for the intellectual left or of inner-city politics anymore. It has expanded in our collective thought to other social spheres thus shedding light more broadly on inequalities by race and gender, both historically and worldwide.

Against the recent backdrop of the Black Lives Matter movement, which began as a protest against police brutality, the focus has largely broadened to other social inequalities, including historical discrimination against communities of colour that have become systemic.

Numerous incidents of historical injustices are known, and others have been revealed in recent times. Examples of such injustices that have had long-term implications on communities today include:

- The Atlantic Slave Trade: 10–15 million people were packed into ships without their consent and sent across the ocean to do nothing but be treated like animals and work and be beaten until they died. And then their children, and their children's children.

- The Tulsa Massacre of 1921 in Oklahoma, USA, against a suburban black community by white racial mobs. This took place on May 31 and June 1, 1921, when mobs of white residents, some of them deputised and given weapons by city officials, attacked black residents and destroyed homes and businesses in the Greenwood District in Tulsa.
- The forced seclusion of children, of native communities, from their parents in North America and Australia. The children were forced into punitive education programs and were put in crowded residential schools that were meant to eradicate their culture, customs, and traditions.
- Algeria has deported thousands of men, women, and children since January 2018 to Niger and Mali in inhumane conditions, and in many cases without considering their legal status in Algeria or their individual vulnerabilities.

Examples of injustice are too numerous to mention but have occurred all around the world in history and still occur today. No country is untouched by this sort of inhumanity, and so there is no real value in pointing the finger at others, as this provides little in the way of useful reconciliation. We need to learn from mistakes and work to provide a better framework where these types of injustices are less likely to occur.

The social and psychological scars of some of these events, on these communities, are still evident today and include skewed resource distribution and life expectancy. In order to ensure that the future for all people is better, a fundamental change needs to occur via a renewed vision around education.

Developments need to be made sustainable, taught, and viewed <u>in the light of what we have</u>, not what we don't have. Change also needs to be accompanied by social development.

Research has shown that an increase in the Gross Domestic Product (GDP) in countries is not directly proportionate to an increase in social development and welfare of its citizens.

Instead, if increases in Gross Domestic Product (GDP) are not effectively managed, disparities between the rich and poor grow wider. This risks instability in society and even the usurping of governments.

Governments, therefore, could and should consider implementing policies that ensure wider-reaching social safety nets for their populations, such as health insurance and social security in retirement or as a result of job loss.

Building Bridges

No doubt there would be detractors to this line of thought.

Most probably, and notably, they would come from the wealthy and powerful parts of society. There would be people who would say, it's too difficult, too expensive, it's just the way things are, it's human nature, it's a bridge too far!

They would mention every conceivable barrier to protect themselves and their privileged position. They might say they give large sums to philanthropic endeavours, and it would be true, in a way, but the real truth is it's a small percentage of what many of them really have.

Large dollar figures are mentioned in the defence of their position, but when compared to what they have and control, it's often a mere pittance. One million dollars to most people is a fortune but is pocket change to them.

It's beyond belief to accept it's human nature to ignore the desperate cries of starving children.

Of course, nature versus nurture is an ongoing question, and its discussion brings into question education and what we teach our children.

To this, I would say, look at the progress over the last three hundred years, much of which people would have thought madness not so long ago, and is now just part of our everyday life.

Humans have always adapted to, and adopted, new ideas and technologies at a rapid rate. Assertions that we are just a product of nature clearly haven't inhibited our ability to change and build bridges to new, better outcomes.

Look at the money invested in reaching the stars whilst we bury our heads in the sand watching people perish in pain and agony.

Surely the idea of reaching out for the stars and providing decent standards of living for all our people aren't mutually exclusive ideas?

Highly Esteemed Supporters

There have been great people in the 20th Century that have shed great light on man's inhumanity to man. People like Gandhi and Mandela instilled great faith and moved mountains for their people – they did amazing things and have rightly been praised for their efforts against all odds.

Worldwide hosted events such as Live Aid raised many millions for famine relief in Africa. But famine still exists!

Culturally, we all share and give in so many ways. Positive interactions are common with people worldwide. Everywhere you go, anywhere in the world, there is music, art, literature, and sport.

Whilst the medium in which they are portrayed can vary greatly, as do the styles, there is a seemingly overwhelming abundance of songs, art, literature, and sport providing positive commentary on life and how we can, or should, strive for better outcomes and share, care, and love each other more.

Musical examples are too numerous to mention, so I'll mention only two:

- The song "Imagine" by John Lennon and Yoko Ono talks about all the people sharing all the world in peace!
- The song "Where Is the Love" by the Black Eyed Peas asks, amongst other things:

❖ What's wrong with the world?
❖ Why are we all so attracted to the drama?
❖ Why can't we all get along?

These songs are widely loved, and people seemingly want to embrace the ideology, but it is now nearly fifty and twenty years, respectively, since they were written and first performed, and what has changed? We still have war, we still have famine, we still have the drama, and we still have the rich getting richer and the poor getting poorer.

Whilst it is true that the positive sentiments provided in the arts are widespread, they mainly appear to be as accompaniment to life, the entertainment, the "sideshow", or the distraction to give us relief from the never-ending cycle of bad news. The bad news, or the so-called "serious side" of life, that confronts us every day. The Arts and Sport are, perhaps, akin to the comic relief in a Shakespearean tragedy. They just give us a break, allow us to breathe, before we refocus on the ongoing diet of drama and tragedy!

Surely, we cannot sit by and let the efforts of these great people fade into history!

Of course, as mentioned, there would still be greedy people who would not see the benefits for everyone or want to see that bigger picture.

And of course, this is not an overnight solution, but you need to start somewhere.

Perhaps we need to start with questioning what we are teaching in schools and universities

The Generally Bad News

These days, the serious side, or generally bad news, is not only provided every day, it comes every minute of every day and from all corners of the world. There is a huge discrepancy between the things we mostly sing and write about and what we see in the news each day. Why don't the things we love and embrace feature more in what we are fed each day through media channels worldwide?

You could easily be led to believe it's a grim and difficult world out there with little or no hope for the future. But is news really just big business, commercialism, and marketing? Is the primary motivation of news organisations making money, or is it the more noble idea of keeping the people informed? Is what we hear actually news, or is it opinion, slanted one way or another, depending on the author, or the authors' employers' particular points of view?

Should we be challenging our media outlets to provide a fairer view of the world – to assist in educating us by presenting pictures, visions, and examples of things we should or could aspire to instead of the usual endlessly depressing litany of mayhem and disasters that we are fed.

Perhaps the media could be utilised to influence culture in a more positive way!

Conclusion

A new education ideology will need to be developed and implemented over many years.

- There have been so many years of the mentality of greed driven into us that it is systemically ingrained in society, as well as ingrained in an individual sense.
- The prevailing mentality driven by the scarcity definition of Economics which underpins much of our education is leading to undesirable and unnecessary outcomes.

There is no greater joy than to see someone smile when they feel like they are being cared for. There is no greater joy that can be had as in the process of giving.

Aren't we all fundamentally singing from the same hymn sheet? Don't we all want better outcomes for our fellow man, woman, or child, no matter their background, culture, or belief?

This philosophy can only take root if it's included in our education systems. It needs widespread discussion in places of learning.

The time is ripe for an **education revolution**. Our children have a unique opportunity in the history of the world right now.

All the conditions of abundance and plenty exist now. The mechanisms to deliver abundance are here in abundance:

- distribution channels exist now like never before in terms of:
  - goods and services
  - information
  - finance and wealth

The possibility to create a self-sustaining garden of Eden exists now!

However, in economic terms, **supply, although it can, does not meet demand** worldwide! Should the study of Economics (Greed and Scarcity) be abandoned, at least in a macro sense?

Should the definition of Economics be changed to perhaps the following:

'The science that studies human behaviour as a relationship between end results and abundant means.'

As per the proposition derived from Lord Robbins' (1932) scarcity definition of Economics:

- 'If food was plentiful, if there was enough capital in business, if there was abundant money and time – there would not be any scope for studying economics.'

We are at that point now!

A mindset underpinned by thoughts of scarcity leads to greed!
A mindset underpinned by thoughts of abundance leads to liberality and goodwill.

We are currently living in an era where changes are being described as disruption. Commonly held views and ways of doing things are being constantly questioned, changed, and improved.

Surely, fundamental disruption of the education system is not immune.

Published literature from the highly esteemed Harvard Undergraduate programme (revised August 2021) says, 'Ultimately, economists make policy recommendations that they believe will make people better off.' Well, there are many millions of people worldwide waiting anxiously and with bated breath for these economists to deliver on their stated goal.

The Harvard programme goes on to say, 'An undergraduate education in economics focuses on learning to analyse the world in terms of trade-offs and incentives – that is, to think like an economist.'

Does our contemporary world need that kind of thinking? Do we want the most influential amongst us thinking with those sorts of constraints and viewing the world through that sort of lens?

*The scarcity definition of Economics is **no longer valid** as we now live in an Age of Abundance*

It is no longer a question of can we have a fairer, more equitable world anymore; it's a question of how and when?

Further, the idea of overwhelming abundance can be discussed, quantified, and measured.

Students of economics, politics, business studies, and social sciences everywhere should be challenging their tutors, teachers, and professors by asking the questions:

Do we still live in a world that should be guided by definitions of scarcity?
and if not,

a) how and when are we going to collectively stand up and say it's an absolute disgrace how enormous amounts of wealth are hoarded by so few?

and

b) how and when are we going to share this wealth and raise the standard of living for all those in dire need to a decent and humane level?

From my perspective, I recommend a more positive underlying theme be studied:

The Study of Abundance.

Imagine.